AN 18 YEARS OLD WIDOW

ABDUL KALAM A

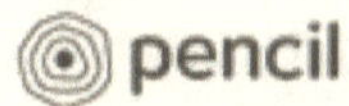

ISBN 978-93-5610-559-1

Published in India 2022 by Pencil

A brand of
One Point Six Technologies Pvt. Ltd.
123, Building J2, Shram Seva Premises,
Wadala Truck Terminal, Wadala (E)
Mumbai 400037, Maharashtra, INDIA
E connect@thepencilapp.com
W www.thepencilapp.com

Author biography

ABDUL KALAM A, is a passionate writer of humanly emotions. He is also a veterinarian by profession and published three works namely, **"Diary of Pain- chapter 1", "Diary of pain chapter-2"** and **"Uncertain lives".**

CONTENTS

At 14,.. 8

Foreword

Dedicated to voiceless **Wonder women ...**

Introduction

In every girl's childhood, they wish many things. They wish to become a doctor, a teacher, a pilot or anything but they wished to become something. But some situations make their entire life miserable. Some fears of her parents like "What if she gets ruined, if we let her study? What if she loves someone, if we let her study? What if she gets abused by someone? What if she gets raped? What if? What if?......." Though those fears were reasonable to themselves, they always forget one thing that she too a has a life, she too has dreams, she too has emotions, needs, etc... Many girls like Asifa, lost their life completely even before starting it. Every girl of her age wishes to be loved, to be cared, to be intimated, to be possessed, etc. Every girl of any age wishes to breathe freely, sit freely, sleep freely, roam freely, or at least talk and sing freely. Many of their wishes remain as only wishes for the rest of their life. Many boys unknowingly have dominance over their opposite gender either their sister, mother, friend, lover, unknown or any relationship they could name it.They unintentionally or intentionally impose their dominance in all ways like with whom they talk, what they talk, how they dress, what to eat, when to sleep, and moreover every activity of her though they name all these as care and possessiveness. Even that is the case, none of the boys thinks that she too has a life and she has her own way to do all things. They forget that she too wishes to do all things as she likes. She never wishes to have a baby on her hand at the age of having books and friends beside her. She never needed to be cared, to be loved, to be possessed by snatching her complete freedom. Leave her, let her live to the fullest. Of course, she wants a life partner but everyone should understand that it is not her need. She doesn't want someone to live with, she needs someone to live with her. Every girl is a unique superpower and no one should miss use it. No one needs to be a feminist to talk all these, one just needs to be a human to understand this.

At 14,

It was a math period then. She was writing down those written on that blackboard. She was excited as the next period was playtime. Bell rang. Math teacher stood up to leave the class.And everyone stood to say,

"Thank you, teacher." in chorus.
Before the teacher stepped out, Office boy entered the class and gave a bit of paper to her. She read that and informed,
"Asifa, you are asked to go home. Take your bag, inform the office and leave. Others may go to the ground."
She left the class, went to the office and saw her uncle standing at the gate. She had no clue. She relieved gate pass and joined her Uncle, who was there to take her home. She asked her Uncle pitifully,
"Uncle, shall I come next period. This is our playtime."
Her uncle shouted,
"Shut up! Just come with me."
Both boarded an auto-rickshaw. The auto stopped in front of her home and there was a gathering. About 50 men and women were standing outside and she was staring at the door. Both stepped out of the auto and she quickly walked inside. When she entered by infiltrating through the gathering, as soon as she stepped inside the home and looked over there, she knelt down with a huge cry on her

eyes and heart. She screamed, she cried. Everyone around her was paying their deep condolences by holding her hands and feeling pity for her. She sat beside the bed but her screams were not ceasing. It was her dad lying on the bed and everyone was looking at him for the very last time one after another. Since her mom passed away a long back after delivering a sister to her, her dad was the one to look after both. Everyone felt so pity for her. She had no siblings except her small sister who was about 5 years old then. The funeral ceremony began. All men left the house by taking his father's coffin on their shoulders.

Men in chorus shouted, "Kalima shahadadh."

Every woman there tried to control her as she was screaming outrageously, "Abba..."

That day evening, as all the funeral ceremony were over and many of the guests were already left, her Uncle, who was her mom's only brother and his family who had love and pity for that family stayed back. Her younger sister was crying either of hunger or missing her dad. As her dad loved his kids so much, he feared to marry another woman. He spent his whole life just for his kids. Everyone there felt bad for those two girls. Shelifted her sister and went inside to feed her. As soon as she went, her Uncle, his family and some other close relatives started to talk about what should be happening next.

Oneof them, "Girl has grown up and lost her mom and dad. Her sister too a small kid. How will they manage to live hereafter?"

Another "We have to do something for them. What about any small shops or seeking any job for her?"

"Girl has grown up. If we let her do any job, she would get spoilt and all the blame would fall on us."

"So, is it fair to leave her just like that?"
"Perhaps, let's raise a fund from all our family and deposit in her account. So that whenever she needs money, let her take."
"Don't even think like that. We are seeing many girls of this generation running away with someone taking all the money. We should not give her such a chance."
"So, what shall we do now?"
"I think, it's better to get her married as soon as possible."
"She is too young to get married. Even if we do so, who will marry her? Nowadays, it too difficult to search for a groom even for a well-settled family. We all know her condition as of now. In the last few months, they even struggled to buy foods as her father fell sick. I only helped them with money and stuff." her Uncle said with a sad face and a big pride.
Oneold lady among them stated, "I know a groom. He is just 29 years old. He is a driver and earns nearly 10000 per month. A few months ago, he met with an accident and he lost his wife.Now, his family members are searching for a bride for him. If you are okay with that, I'll request them to marry her without any dowry. Nowadays, marrying without dowry is so rare."
"He is too old, Chachi. She is too young and how can we let her marry an already married one? There is a gap of moreover 15 years between them. How could they marry and livetogether?"
Chachi replied, "I got married when I was 13 and my husband was 28 years old then. Ain't I living happily? Everything is possible. Just say "yes," I'll do rest of the things. Already married men knows well how to keep her happy than the unmarried one."

"Would you let your granddaughter marry a man like him?"

"Why should I? My granddaughter has her father and mother and also she has properties on her name now itself. I said it only to help her as she has nothing with her. Tell me straight if I don't need to say anything. You do on your own. Who listens to the good I say...?" Chachi whispered herself.

Her uncle replied, "Nothing like that Chachi. I thought she is too young. And doubted whether she could able to run a family." he paused.

After a minute of silence, he again, "Let me ask her once for her decision."

His wife from behind questioned, "If she says "No", would you take her to our home along with you?" She gazed at him in a threatening manner.

He got scared of her tone and said, "Okay. Let's leave it to God's will. Anyway, you ask for them about the alliance. Let's see what is about to happen."

HerUncle entered home and neared her to say that she was going to get married soon. She was shocked and had no idea to say anything. She was speechless as she yet did not overcome her father's death. He just informed and left. She had no idea about what marriage is and did not know what changes that would bring in her life. She just felt that she couldn't go to school anymore and would not able to meet her friends after that. She was so tender that she felt too bad of thinking that she couldn't play in her school playtime anymore. She felt so insecure that the one with whom she would get married would sleep next to her instead of her father who slept in between his two kids. Her father's death depressed her on one side and the fear of something that was about to happen depressed her on the other side. She, an innocent soul was sandwiched between these two which destroyed her completely. She felt so shattered. She felt so lost.

The next day morning, some of her friends came to pay their condolences and to give some hope to her. When they arrived, she cried hugging them. They all tried to convince her and also tried to comfort her by giving their shoulders to cry. After taking a few breaths, she revealed that she was going to get married. She sobbed eiither because of the marriage or because of her father's death, only she knows. Her friends were shocked and asked her whether they need to inform their teachers so that they would help her to stop the marriage. But she denied and said that it was the only way she had, to live and look after her sister. All fellows broke and left after some time.

A month passed. Groom's family wished to make engagement and fix the marriage date. They planned for engagement and prepared lunch and sweets for the groom's family. Till that she and her sister were taken care of by her Uncle. Her Aunt taught her the marital things, do's and don't. She taught to cook a variety of dishes and how to respect her mother-in-law and father-in-law. She advised her to learn about the family as soon as she enters their home. She said not to go against their decision and not to say "No" for any of their commands. She was advised to tolerate her husband at any cost and said that husband has every right even to kill their wife. Meanwhile, her Uncle called Aunt to add some more sugar in sweets, she threatened her that he would die if she adds more sweet. Looking at them, she smiled. On seeing her smile, her Aunt said, if you are enough talented to make your husband fall for you, you will be like a queen as I am. Though she couldn't understand actually what she was saying, she nodded for her every statement.

Andthe day came for the engagement ceremony. The groom along with his family and relatives entered their home. Everyone sat down, had tea and sweets, talked about good and bad, weather and work, informed officially that it would be the second marriage for the groom and started to talk about expenses and dowry.One among the Groom's family,

"We don't need any dowry. Send only your girl to our home and we'll look after her like our own daughter."

Her Uncle, "Sure, I know you'll treat her as your daughter. But I guess you'll have two daughters instead." with a laugh hiding his insecurity.

Groom'sfather: "We have no objection for no dowry. But we can't take her sister with us. Our house is not capable of accommodating her as we are already short of rooms."

Her Uncle replied, "She is still a small girl and also she won't live without her sister. She'll be searching for her always. Please consider to take along with her."

"We felt pity for her and decided to give a life for her. But we are not so generous to feel pity for her sister too. You keep the child with you till she grows up and I'll help you to find a Groom for her, even I will give my share for her marriage."

It was moreover like an argument it went. Finally, they decided to take her sister along with her with a condition.

"Okay! We'll feed and grow her but the house they are staying should be registered on my son's name."

"Of course, the property they possess will surely come to your daughter-in-law. There is no doubt in that. But her sister too has a share in the property. So let's register the house on both of them so that when she grows up she might get her share."

"We can't accept that. The land must be registered on him so that we'll feed her for that share."

With no other ways and no more patience or with no sort of care or having a relieved stress of getting rid of them, her Uncle accepted their call. Then came the talk about expenses. This time her Uncle's voice raised. He said that they should accept all the expenses as he accepted to give land to them. As they planned to do marriage in a very simple manner, they accepted and marked a date for marriage.

At15,

After a month, she turned 15, and her marriage was decided on the next day of her birthday though no one knew. Every year on her birthday, her father used to wake her up and wished her as a first-person. He used to tell her to pray first and eat some sweets. Her day was somehow extraordinary every year. She used to get wishes from her friends in school, chorus

"Happy birthday" song by every class she visits to distribute chocolates, hand- drawn greetings by close friends and ended with a dinner of sweets and biryani. That day, as usual, she woke up early in the morning with a smile on her face thinking of her birthday and heard her father's advise to pray though it was an illusion. She prayed as her father's will and ate a spoon of sugar, not knowing that the next day would be the last day of her childhood. Actually, she did not know the depth meaning of anything. But she decided to enter into that kind of life which she never even dreamt of. She did not even mature enough to think fantasies of marriage, children, a new family, a new environment like most of the girls after their adolescence do. She did not even think of marriage before rather than wishing to get married. That day, she was locked up in a room in the name of rites. She was not allowed to talk with any of her friends in the thought that anyone could change her mind. She was not worried about the marriage the next day but felt sad about not getting wishes from her best friends. Her Uncle came with a cup of sweet towards her. Her face blossomed. A thousand butterflies flew at once in her belly. She was so happy. When he bowed the cup towards her and said to take it, she felt so happy.

Shereplied, "Thanks, Uncle. Only you did not forget my birthday."

HerUncle's face turned sad and felt pity for her.

He replied, "Its rites to feed bride with sweets, dear. Anyway happy birthday."

Her face turned so disappointed with no instance. She refused to eat the sweet and laid down again on the bed. With those memories, she slept. By afternoon, she was taught to wear saree. She looked so gorgeous in the saree and looked like a typical bride though she was not so tall and not yet grown fully. She was then a bride except by her heart as she was a child yet. Till that day evening, she kept on wearing, again and again, all those 14 sarees which included her mom's too. She kept on wearing until she got tired of and felt like fainting. That night, a group of ladies who were her relatives, sat around her and they were telling about the way she should behave with her husband. They told her to go by his wishes and to never hesitate to do what he asked her to do. They told her not to talk against him, not to rage at him and even if he beat her, they told not to get angry and leave the home at any cost. That said her to tolerate anything he does even if it hurt her. She nodded to all their advice. Later that night, after most of then slept, three old women entered her room where she was left alone. They wished to tell some secrets about the bed matters to her. Though she understood everything partially, she nodded again and again. They took her to the bathroom and one of them carried a pair of scissors to clear her pubic hairs which also was told as a rite. She never did that before as her mom was not with her as she died three years before her puberty. She was about to scream not knowing exactly what was happening to her. In fact, she screamed but one of those three held her mouth tight so that no one could hear. After removal of those hairs, they made her bath with turmeric and shikakai. She felt fear for the first time but did not know why. Next day, she was set to go to see her husband for the first time. But by rite, she should be allowed to see her husband on the marriage day only after marriage that is the Groom must sign the register in the mosque and the bride must sign the register in the function hall that is her home, where the function had been organised. Before signing the register by the bride, police arrived on hearing news of minor girl's marriage. Everyone there was tensed up and shocked. By luck or some kind of pre-plan, her Uncle prepared a duplicate birth certificate for her dating three years earlier to her actual date of birth. On hearing news of police arrival, she was told to say that she completed high school last year. When she was asked by the policemen, she repeated what she was taught to. Though the police did not believe, they bribed them for three thousand rupees and a box of biryani and sweets. They, by hard luck, escaped from them and she, by her fate, trapped in that.

Afterthe signing ceremony, sweets were distributed and both the bride and groom we're made to sit beside, everyone wished and blessed them and a few gifted them with money and gifts. She did not utter a word to him, neither he. She actually did not utter even a word from the morning to anyone. All rituals we're completed except the first night. That night, she was prepared as a feast to a devil of moreover his father's age. She entered the room and he was already waiting there. For the first time, she looked at his face clearly. He was about 35-40 years of age physically though 30 years old actually. He had a huge body with dark skin, gruff voice and partially bald. His tummy touched his thighs. In front of him, she looked like a deer as prey to the hippo. As soon as she looked at his face, her heartbeat went out of pace. She trembled the next step. She managed to sit beside him. He touched her cheeks. She felt so insecure and nervous. She turned away her face. With his rough hands, he grabbed her hair and made her see him. She was afraid like seeing a wild boar in front. When the pressure from his hands increased, she couldn't bear and she started to cry. He talked his first word to her for the first time.

He shouted, "Didn't they tell you what to do?"

She couldn't answer as her throat held tight of fear. She cleared her throat but did not utter. She closed her eyes because of fear of getting hurt. With no other words, he touched her lower tummy and crushed so hard with the other hand. She couldn't bear the pain. But she remembered those things told by those grannies. She remained silent by closing her eyes and mouth so tight. He did not cuddle, show love, handle her with care but he was wild. He forcefully removed her dress and also had himself undressed. She resisted but he forced. She cried but he did not leave. As he pulled out all her clothes she covered her body with her hands. He smooched her so hard and wild. She did not know what would happen next but remained crying as she had no way to go out. For some time she was able to resist him but he was too wild to resist. Then, he tried to penetrate his manhood on her famine part. She cried out loud as she couldn't bear the pain but he did not leave. She pleaded him to leave but he did not. She screamed so loud that her screams were heard out, but no one came to rescue her. He did what he wished to do but when he started doing it, she fainted but he did not stop. She bled heavily but he did not stop. She was speechless but he did not stop. She was unconscious but he did not mind. When he had his orgasm, he held his fingers near her nose just to check the breathing. She was breathing but not conscious. He slapped her so hard on her cheeks, she did not reply. Then, he just fell asleep after spreading a blanket over her naked body.

The dark sky faded. The red started to appear not only in the sky but also in her life. The red was not only the color from the sun but also from the blood she shed. She was unable to get up. She felt like a nightmare. She was lying on the bed the whole morning with only a blanket over her body. Her legs felt numb to move. At about 11 am, she managed to get up, rolled a cloth over her and decided to take bath. The way to the bathroom was so hard for her to walk. She slipped many times as her leg couldn't bear the pain. She held the wall to support her walk. Every step she walked, she felt like dying. For every step, she cried and called her parents to take her along with them. She pleaded God to either not give her pain or give strength to bear the pain or at least the death. She lived in the hell for those steps. After taking a bath, she again sat on her room and thought of her school and friends. She thought of her mom and dad. She cried. He went to work but she did not know when he left. She felt hungry and ate those fruits kept there. She did not move but wept.

It was about 5 in the evening and everyone from the Groom's side got ready to leave to their house. She was sitting on her bed as she couldn't move. Her friend visited at her house. As soon as she saw her, she hugged and cried like a baby seeing her mother after a serious kidnap. She cried hard. She screamed. She told her all the things that happened last night. Her friend too cried with her. She asked her to leave him and to come to her house so that her parents could look after her. But she said, "If I leave, no one would look after my sister. My fate is decided but I did not know that would be this cruel. Anyway, I suffered a lot and no one can change that now. Don't let any girl of our age suffer like me. Now I have to leave this house. Maybe I would return to this house as soon as the documents of this house registered on him. Let's see again if I'm alive."

Sheleft after leaving tears and with a broken heart.At that late evening, everyone left and her home became orphan with no one to look after. She made her little sister sit on her thighs and she sat beside him on the bus. For a week, she stayed in her mother-in-law's home and every night she experienced the hell as same as the first night. Every day after they both entered the room to sleep, without any notification or any kind of gestures, he used to pull her dress away from her body and started to humiliate her, abuse her, beat her and literally raped her. Every night for a week she screamed and begged to leave but his ears did not catch her words. She eventually fainted as she couldn't bear the pain. Her body got many scratches and wounds but no one cared. After a week, she got used to it. She did not fell unconscious but mentally absent all the time. He did not leave her every single night except the times of her menstruation as he was aware that it might lead her to death. She was haunted and ferociously raped many times by the same person. She feared to look his face. A week later, they both shifted their things and clothes to her own house which was literally his thereafter. That day night, he drank too much. Till that day, she did not know he would drink. He entered home, her sister was playing with some small toys. As soon as, he saw her sister, he whacked her hard enough with his barefoot that she cried so badly. When she tried to stop, he whacked her too. That night, both were crying and he ate his food and entered the room. He called her but she said that she was feeding her sister and would come after she putting her to sleep. When he listened to those replies, with no time, he came out and slammed the plate she was holding to feed her. Food spilt all over the dining hall. He grabbed her head and pulled her inside the room. Her sister, an innocent soul, picked up that food dropped on the floor and ate to beat her hunger. This became routine and daily she faced a hell.

Twomonths passed. His parents visited their home to ask for any good news. When they heard nothing that is she was not pregnant yet, they cursed her and ordered her to get them a grandson soon. He gave them some money which was happening every month and after having a meal they left. She did not have enough money to buy anything for her sister and for herself too. She was afraid to ask him for money thinking he would beat her. With the help of a neighbor and womenself- help group, she found a job for her. She had to assemble writing pen in return she got 10 rupees for a thousand pens. After her husband left, she used to do from the morning to evening. For a day, she managed to assemble 3000- 4000 pens which was so less when compared to others. She saved all that money daily without her husband's knowledge. She fulfilled her need and also her sister's with that money. Their needs are not so expensive as it was readily available at any smallshops that had sweets and chocolates, sanitary napkins, soap and other utilities.

Months passed. She asked her husband to let her sister go to school, but he refused. She asked again and again, but every time she received only hurt and vulgar words for which she did not even know the meaning. But she did not quit. She denied to get in bed but he brutally raped her. She denied to cook food, he stopped to buy cereals and stuff for home. For days, she was able to manage food expenses with her earning but it was not enough for the whole week. She was determined to send her to school. For that, she made her heart so cruel and with extreme agony, she admitted her in an ashram and looked after her needs and requirements for school by earning from her job. She used to visit her once in a week and did not let her husband know where she was admitted. He beat her so many times to reveal where she is, but she feared that he would hurt her so she did not reveal to him. She was brutally beaten most of the times. But she remained calm. Later he did not bother about her as he thought without

her, expenses would be reduced.
Itwas about 6 months since her marriage. She understood him but he did not. She did everything before he asked to. From serving food to rubbing his back while bathing. She did everything with utmost fear that he would hurt her. She was afraid of getting beaten by him. She sacrificed herself, her childhood, her happiness and everything but he did not even consider her sacrifices. One day, she fainted and fall on the ground while going to fetch water from the municipality pipe. People around there saw her and took her to the hospital. The doctor informed that she was pregnant and also said that her uterus was so weak to carry a child as she was so young. She advised her to take extra care and not to strain more. She smiled not because of the happiness but sarcastically because of the word "No more straining" thinking of her daily life. She informed her Uncle and family and also her MOTHER-IN-LAW. All were so happy to hear but this news did not affect her husband anyway until she delivered a baby. She said those words uttered by the doctor to him. He just stared and went off. From then, she took utmost care of herself. She went to regular checkups monthly though her husband never accompanied her.

At 16,

Months passed. She was about six months pregnant then. That day, it was her birthday. She woke up early in the morning with a smile on her face. Her husband was not beside her as he already went away to deliver a load. She prayed early morning like her dad said and ate a spoon full of sugar. Her best friend visited her to wish "Happy birthday" which made her feel that she was still alive and she got surprised to see her tummy swollen. After wishing birthday greetings, she congratulated on her pregnancy. She again smiled the same smile that she smiled with the doctor. That smile was so frustrated and lifeless. That smile had several deep pains buried. That smile was not so easy to differentiate from the normal one just by sight but had an infinite difference from the normal one. After an hour of talk, she left her home. She, with the thought of her past memories, lost herself. She smiled occasionally just only because of her memories. She lived only because of her memories and only for her child that was yet to be born.Whenever she felt tired of her life, she used to keep her hands over her belly considering her son's head and massaged slowly by saying a few words.

She said, "Paapa, Ammi lives only for you. You are the one who will change my fate. You are the one who will cure my pain. I don't know what to say, but I'm sure that I will live only for you. Don't get a fate like your mom.Write your own fate beautifully."

Though she did not know what to say, she used to say like that. She said those words repeatedly whenever she felt like talking to her kid. Those words unknowingly boosted some sort of confidence in her and she determined to live anyways suffering any pain for her child's sake. She built a lot of dream about him. And also neither because of the kid she loved nor because of what she got from her husband, she built a thought in her heart that however, he abused her, even though brutally, he would love his child for sure. Though he beat her daily, he never let her starve. Though he all the time rages against her, she felt he never hated and sent her out of the house. There is a minor difference between dominance and hate and she felt it.

Though he did not make her smile and never missed to hurt her, he did not let her feel insecure. For the first time, she felt happy with what she got. She prayed God just to let this life go on its own way without any loss anymore. She thanked God for the first time after years as he was not hurting her much because of the baby in her tummy looked out like a huge bump.

Months passed. She was at her last stage of pregnancy and the doctor reminded her to be extra careful as her uterus was so weak.The doctor advised that operation would be safe for both mother and the infant but the whole family refused. That day, she got pain and her bag of waters leaked while she was cooking at home. She was unable to stand and grabbed support to sit. She screamed outrageously. Luckily a neighbor heard her scream and admitted her in the hospital. They had no choice but to operate. Her screams were uncontrollable. Doctors sedated her and brought the child out by operation. She was about to die after that delivery as her pulse and heartbeat dropped below critical point. Somehow doctors managed to save her and advised her family and her husband to take good care of her as she was so weak. She delivered a baby boy and everyone in her family was happy, even her husband too. He lifted his child and smiled at him. That was the first time she looked at him smiling. His parents were happy to see a boy. No one knew what would have happened if it was a girl. She did not even think of it. For the first time, her husband smiled at her. She felt goosebumps for the first time in a long while. Some sort of odd feeling boosted all over the body which never happened before. She felt happy for the first time by seeing him. As she was so young her breastscouldn't secrete enough milk for the child, doctors prescribed Breast milk substitutes and also advised to feed her properly for good milk secretion. After three days of bed rest, she was taken to the home. Though her husband did not talk to her, he bought fruits and food daily. On seeing those fruits, she felt that he too had some kind of kindness in him. She felt surprised by seeing him at the times he looking and laughing at the baby or kissing him. He was tamed by the baby and her thought came true that is the baby would reduce her pain. He was completely unrecognizable at the times he was with his child. Though he did not take care of her or talked some good words to her, his love towards her child added meaning for her life. At the times, he goes to work, she used to take her child to visit her little sister. Her sister, a little soul, was too excited and happy about seeing the child. She used to kiss him, play with him and talk with him with that little chick voice. On seeing that, Asifa's eyes would drain tears. Those meetings were so short lived but happiness was endless. At the time, when Asifa had to leave, her sister used to cry a lot. She with tears draining in her eyes left that place.Months passed. From the sixth month of baby, she started to feed him with multi grain health mix as recommended by the doctor. Whenever the baby cries, she used to feed him with that as her breasts couldn't secrete enough milk then. Meantime, while she fed the baby with that, she too unknowingly ate that as it was so sweet and pleasantly smelled of roasted grains. As the pack was used up so frequently, her husband doubted. One day, he came to the home earlier and she was feeding the baby. He was at the door and she did not know his arrival. He watched her feeding the baby and felt so moved by her as she too ate her baby's food. He felt so bad for his actions towards her though he did not stop to dominate. He entered home and she was shocked to see him with a spoon full of health mix in her mouth. She was afraid of thinking that he would beat her for sure.

Instead, he smiled at her and said, "If you wish to eat, just eat. We can buy somemore."

She was surprised by his words and smiled awkwardly in return. He slowly started being nice to her though did not spoke any lovely or caring words to her. He bought snacks frequently and made a check on her health too. She, like a child, finished all the snacks alone during the time he was not at home. She took the utmost care of her baby. She dressed him in the way she liked to dress herself or the Barbie doll that she used to dress up during her childhood. She bought many makeup kits for him like baby powder, baby soap, baby shampoo, moisturizer, eyebrow pencils, and much more for her kid. As those things were for his child, he too did not bother about that unless it was unnecessary expenses.

At 17,

She was about 3 months pregnant again then. Her husband this time took almost care for her that is, he accompanied on her routine check-up every month and duly bought medicines for her. But his dominance was not ceased even then. If he found any guilt of her like making extra expenses other than that she spent for her baby, raising voice against him or talking with any neighbors, he would beat her for sure. She started to love her life as it was fully dedicated to her children. She completely stopped to worry about herself, her health, pain and happiness. Her thoughts all day was only about her child, one in her hand and the other in her belly. She frequently thought about her sister and wept like a baby all the time. She requested his permission to get back her sister to their home so that she would be helpful for her. As she carried his another child on the belly, he did not refuse though at first, he got angry for hiding her from him so many months. Same day, she went to the ashram and brought back her sister to home after all formalities. Her sister hugged her belly as it was slightly enlarged because of the kid inside.When she hugged her belly, she felt immense happiness did not know why. Her sister was about 7 years old then. She said all the stories happened in that ashram from the day one since she left. Her words expressed some feel of longing for care and love which she quickly understood as she too was longing for that unknowingly. She and her sister used to play games like 5 stones, pallanguzhi and much more that they played during their childhood. She completely forgot that she was a mother a child and played like an actual child. When her sister was near her, she literally became her companion or partner in all activities and did all those childish things by even forgetting that she was pregnant then. That day, she was doing her pen work and her sister was helping her. A cadaver van stopped in front of their house and the horn sounded again and again.

She stopped her work, went out and asked them, "Whom do you want?"

They confirmed the address with her and asked her to check whether she knows the person, dead inside. She had no idea about what they were talking about. She walked to rear side of the van and for her each step her heart bounced. When they opened the door, she looked at that cadaver. At the instant, she gazed at it, she was short of her breath, energy and everything. It was her husband died on the road accident. At that instant, she did not cry but fainted on the road. Meanwhile, everyone near her house gathered. Some of them took her to hospital and some of them took care of the cadaver and prepared for the funeral ceremony. With that shock, she had a miscarriage and lost her unborn child.All relatives and people of their hometown visited to see him for the last time. After she was discharged from hospital that evening, his funeral ceremony and her widow rites happened simultaneously. She was shattered from her heart. She became helpless, speechless and miserable. She did not cry rather depressed too much thinking about the future of her kid. She did not worry about her but about her sister and kid. Her Uncle after the funeral gave some cash to her to make her living. That day, late evening, his funeral rites were completed and her bangles we're broken, her ornaments were removed and naming her as a 'Widow' was done. She did nothing but broken and sat at the corner of the house with her kid on her lap. Then, that night, every close relative sat together to discuss what should happen next as she had a year old kid with her. Her mother-in-law was asked to take responsibility for her but she did not agree to them to make her stay in their home.

Shesaid, "Our son only fed us these days. We don't have any source of income. How will we be able to feed her and her sister?"

Her Uncle, "Is it fair that you telling these words? We gave her to you and now she is your responsibility. You must look after her. She is a poor little girl though."

"Whatever you say, we don't have enough resource to

accommodate her with us. If you have so much care for her, make her stay in your house."

HerAunt, "How would be that possible? We are here just to help her, not to feed your daughter-in-law or your grandson. If that is the case, we will take her little sister with us. You take your grandson and your daughter in law."

Hearing all these conversations from being inside the home, Asifa came out and shouted, "No one needs to look after me and my sister. We know to look for ourselves. You people just shut your mouth and get out soon."

On hearing her words, her Uncle got tensed up and raised his arm to slap her. When his hand was about to reach her cheek, she grabbed his hand and said, "You have no more right to raise your hand at me. I know to live on my own. You mind your own business. Now, everyone get out!" she screamed.

With those words, he left that house with his wife and kids by saying that he would never see her face again even if she dies. Other people over there started to whisper about her. She being already broken to the core, did not care about those whispers but entered home, locked herself inside the room and cried, cried and cried like hell. Her cry was so loud that heard from outside to her sister and kid which made them cry too.

At that night, it was about 11, she remembered that they both did not eat from the afternoon. So she prepared food for them and woke them up to eat. With the money left in her hand, she managed to pass that month and from the next month, everything changed like never before. She was not allowed in any functions. She was not allowed to talk with unmarried young girls. Even her best friends were restricted by their parents to meet her. She was looked like a stroke of bad luck by all. After that month, she was unable to fetch food for her kid and sister. She had no one to go and ask for help. They were literally orphaned. Her baby cried of hunger and her sister too. She too couldn't bear hunger. She sought help from the neighborhood for a few days. As they felt pity for her, they provided her with food and milk. About a week, her neighbor provided her but later they started to treat her very rude with pleasing words. They expected her to do their households like washing clothes, cleaning floor and kitchen utensils in return for their help. At first, being a kid, she washed all their clothes and did all works requested by them. For about a week it continued. The request became orders. She was forced to do all their household works. Over the day, men in her neighbor's house where she did maiden works, started to touch her on cheeks and over the head when his wife was not at home. In the beginning, she did not know the intension of those touches as he was respectable of her father's age. But later, He used to stare her while she was washing clothes and sweeping home. She felt insecure but she did anyway just to ensure the next meal for her kid and sister. Day by Day, she was literally treated as a maiden and respect for her was questioned.

Oneday, while she was wrapping bedsheets over the bed in their home, he came inside the bedroom without her notice. While she was bending over the bed to adjust the bedcover, he appeared behind her and suddenly grabbed her hip and pulled her back towards him. She was so much frightened. Her whole body and soul were too much terrified. She tried to escape forward but he did not leave. She turned around her body and slapped him very hard that he took off his hand from her hip. She cried. She tried to run away but he ran after to the room door and blocked her. He, without any second thought, fell on her feet and pleaded not to say anyone. He threatened that if she revealed that to anyone he would put himself to death. He begged her saying that whatever happened before was happened unknowingly. She without a word left the place and never looked back there even when she was called by his wife many times. She was too much hurt by that incident and decided not to trust any men anymore. She cried a lot and feared to enter another's house. By heart, she became so weak. It became her worst nightmare ever. She lost her only source of food and decided to find a job for herself as she wished not to die because of starvation.

Meanwhile, she searched for a job throughout the city. She went to every shop down there though she was filled with fear and insecurities. Some of them refused to offer a job as there were many other men working and that too she was young. Many of them refused just because she was a widow. Finally, she went to a clinic to seek a job as a cleaner or maid women. The doctor there was so generous and kind-hearted and also there were few other women working as nurse and pharmacist. So her insecurities were compromised and she had a hope that she would not suffer anymore. He offered her the job of an assistant nurse. Her job was to help the nurse with disposing of the medical wastes, cleaning and sanitizing the clinic after the duty hours. She was paid a salary of 3000 per month for it though it was too low to run a family these days. From morning 8 to evening 5 she had to work there and her little sister took care of her kid. Everything went well for some days. People of that rubbish society

started to whisper again.
Someof them told, “It's been only three months since she lost her husband! She's starting to live happily."
Some others said, “She surely will become Stepney of that doctor. She must have bewitched him to get that job.”
Manyothers talked in many different ways. Those words were senseless, ruthless, cutthroat and harmful words that anyone could say to others. Many of them called her slut, bitch, whore and much more when they saw her with any other male even though she talked only on account of work or formal things and also when she rejected many men’s approach. She, a poor little kid, was only able to resist those words entering her mind. But every night before sleep, every word about her, she heard that day haunted her like ghost dreams. She cried every night but every morning she started with a smile on her kid and a talk with her sister. Many men knowing her financial and social condition approached her for one night stands and long term ‘keep’ for their lust. On hearing those words, her childish young soul was hurt a lot. She died each and every second. Over days, she encountered many men approaching her and many calls to her mobile number which the doctor gifted her for office and emergency purpose. She was about to explode every time. Many of the calls to her mobile number started with a question, “How much do you cost?”
She, an innocent soul, thereafter, afraid to attend any call. Those calls were made by the men and their friends of whom she rejected. But she never thought of any men in her life again. Though she was humiliated and abused so much, she never complained to anyone about that as she feared that would affect her kid and sister. Many boys of

their early twenties and late teens, not aware of her married and widowed status, they proposed her to fall in love. Whenever she was exposed to that kind of proposal, she reminded her school days where the word 'love' was seen as the most exciting and pleasure-giving word. She smiled sarcastically inside her and rejected them without a word. Her life moved on with no solution for those things. Whenever she encounters girls of herage going to college first year and enjoying their college life, her childish soul envied and wished to live just a day like that. But when her kid and sister's face flashed in her mind, her wishes faded and she comes back to the reality. However, she was so strong and determined on the decision of growing her kid into a nice successful HUMAN. She wished to give a good education, good manners, discipline and wished to see him as a doctor. She lives with the same hope and determination that her son would become a most respectable person one day. She is living. She is living for her kid. She is living. She is living for her sister. She is living...

In every girl's childhood, they wish many things. They wish to become a doctor, a teacher, a pilot or anything but they wished to become something. But some situations make their entire life miserable. Some fears of her parents like "What if she gets ruined, if we let her study? What if she loves someone, if we let her study? What if she gets abused by someone? What if she gets raped? What if? What if?......." Though those fears were reasonable to themselves, they always forget one thing that she too a has a life, she too has dreams, she too has emotions, needs, etc... Many girls like Asifa, lost their life completely even before starting it. Every girl of her age wishes to be loved, to be cared, to be intimated, to be possessed, etc. Every girl of any age wishes to breathe freely, sit freely, sleep freely, roam freely, or at least talk and sing freely. Many of their wishes remain as only wishes for the rest of their life. Many boys unknowingly have dominance over their opposite gender either their sister, mother, friend, lover, unknown or any relationship they could name it.They unintentionally or intentionally impose their dominance in all ways like with whom they talk, what they talk, how they dress, what to eat, when to sleep, and moreover every activity of her though they name all these as care and possessiveness. Even that is the case, none of the boys thinks that she too has a life and she has her own way to do all things. They forget that she too wishes to do all things as she likes. She never wishes to have a baby on her hand at the age of having books and friends beside her. She never needed to be cared, to be loved, to be possessed by snatching her complete freedom. Leave her, let her live to the fullest. Of course, she wants a life partner but everyone should understand that it is not her need. She doesn't want someone to live with, she needs someone to live with her. Every girl is a unique superpower and no one should miss use it. No one needs to be a feminist to talk all these, one just needs to be a human to understand this.

www.ingramcontent.com/pod-product-compliance
Lightning Source LLC
La Vergne TN
LVHW050429160726
843469LV00041B/1286

9789356105591